I0163340

FROM THE MOUTH OF BABES

How to
Earn & Save
Money

Young People's Handbook
for Economic Discipline

Khalis J. Harris

With illustrations by Mikal Harris

FROM THE MOUTH OF BABES

HOW TO EARN & SAVE MONEY

Young People's Handbook for Economic Discipline

By **Khalis J. Harris**

ISBN-13: 978-0615744735
ISBN-10: 0615744737

Written in 1995
Never published

1st Edition April 2014

© Copyright 2014
W.O.M.B. PUBLICATIONS
Jersey City, NJ

FROM THE MOUTH OF BABES

HOW TO EARN & SAVE MONEY

Young People's Handbook for Economic Discipline

By Khalis J. Harris

Edited by **Raymond Harris**
Cover Art & Illustrations by **Mikal Harris**

Dedication

This book is dedicated to my mother,
Ms. Carolyn Williams, my grandmothers,
the late Mrs. Elizabeth Harris, Mrs. Louise
Sykes and my father, Mr. Raymond Harris.

Thank you all for the life you've given me.

Table of Contents

Preface

My name is Raymond Harris. I am the proud father of Khalis J. Harris, the author of this book. When my son was twelve years old, he came to me and said "Dad, I want to write a book." I told him "whatever you want to do, just get started on it and whatever you need to know as far as information goes, feel free to ask me questions or take from your own experiences. I was a self-employed sales person at the time and he always showed interest in my work, so I would constantly teach him on the principles of business and selling. Little did I know what was stirring in his young but fertile mind, and by age thirteen, he handed me a stack of papers and said "Dad, I finished my book." I was a bit stunned because I didn't expect so much! Well needless to say, it was so good that I vowed to get it published for him. I was so proud!

And then life happened. Between working, getting re-married and starting another family, my good intentions got lost somewhere along the way, but I never once forgot about my promise to him, so I saved that pile of papers for the last 19 years, and they have been moving around with me till this very day. They're all quite brittle but still legible.

What it all boils down to is a very proud father who's trying to keep his word to his son. I now have 6 more boys and 2 girls whom all exemplify various forms of talent. Ironically my 13 yr old son Mikal (something about age 13) did all the illustrations in the book. He is a very promising artist and a bit of a child prodigy himself, as was Khalis, as you'll soon learn while reading on. The information he shares on these pages still holds true today as much as it did 19 yrs ago. No doubt he was ahead of his time.

I truly pray that you'll enjoy reading his book as much as I enjoyed preparing it. It's been such a long time coming and I am very happy that it's finished. The message here to parents is simple; please keep your word to your children no matter how long it may take, because to them a *promise* is and will always be a *promise*.

Raymond Harris- *Editor*

Introduction

So you're probably wondering why a thirteen year old would write a book about how to earn and save money, right? Well it's simple; I just got tired of not having any! I mean, an allowance may be one thing, but it never seems to be enough for the high price stuff that you want to buy as you get older, since prices keep going up. Your parents can only handle but so much with the bills and all, so I thought that I would come up with a way to make my own money. I found out that as long as you're not chicken, and are daring enough to give it a try, there are several ways to earn and save money. Let's face it, if you want something, it's best to try and make a way to get it, because if not you, than someone else will.

That's why I wrote this book, to help young people to realize that we don't have to wait until we're older just to earn and save money. We can make as much as we want to right now, as long as we're willing to work hard for it. I have tried most of the things I'm writing about and believe me, they work. And it can work for all kids no matter where you live; whether you're from America, Japan, China, Africa, Arabia, Spain, the Islands, or the North Pole, anywhere, because most of us kids go through similar experiences, and have the people and the things we need to make money right within our reach.

So take notes as you read through the chapters, and soon you'll see just how easy and rewarding these methods will be, once you give them a try.

Khalis J. Harris- Author
September 1995
Age 13

Chapter One

Help your parents spend less on "Mr. Bill"

"GOOD DAY, MADAM! I'M MR. BILL. I AM HERE TO COLLECT."

Children often go around complaining about never having money. When they go to ask their parents for money, their parents often reply "I'm broke". And do you want to know why? I'll tell you why. It's because if you're like most kids, you probably sit at home and have friends come over to your house to play Sega Genesis, Super Nintendo, Jaguar, CD-Rom and other game systems, which is perfectly normal for kids. What's not normal is that you want to play them all day and all night! The electric bill is going to cost quite a bit of money because you're using up the lights and probably keeping the radio, television, and VCR plugged in and on all night.

You may not realize it but you are helping to run up a very big bill. Your parents have to pay the bills. You shouldn't do that if you want to receive money when you ask for it. You should be smart and say to yourself, "I will cut off every light when I come out of a room, and I will turn the television off when I'm finished watching video games when my friends are over." You'll be helping to cut down on the usual amount of money parents would use for bills. You'll also be allowing your parents the opportunity to have extra money that they'll be happy to share with you because they did not have to spend it all up on bills.

Now you have money and you're happy, but first you must start by being smart enough to ask yourself "Wow, how come my parents never have any extra money?"

You have to start looking at the things they spend their money on and shorten it and make them pay much, much less than what they are paying. Look at all the bills they pay. Ask your parents what bills do they pay and try to cut down on them and help them to pay less.
Here are some of the things that you can help to cut down on:

- *Light and gas bill* (electric bill)
- *Telephone bill* (don't talk 24 hrs. a day)
- *Credit cards* (don't pick the most expensive stuff for them to buy for you)

Most of these you can do something about, but you can't do nothing about the rent. So try it, you'll see after a time that it really works and you'll notice that your parents will have more extra money to give to you the next time you ask for it. Try it and see.

Learn to "Earn" your allowance

There are a lot of ways that you can earn money; such as selling old toys, games or clothes, selling lemonade on a blazing hot summer day, or just doing ordinary chores around the house. Parents love to see their child being mindful of their duties and responsibilities without having to be told to do them, so after you take care of everything you have to do such as taking out the trash, washing the dishes, mowing the lawn (if you're old enough), cleaning up your room, keeping yourself clean, finishing your homework and anything else that you know your parents expect of you, then they'll be glad to give you an allowance if you ask for one. Just think of it like this; those are things you're supposed to do anyway so if you can get paid for doing them, why not? That's how you get things, by getting things done.

You also have to ask often when you go out of the house if anyone needs anything from the store. Even if you are not going out or to the store, ask that question a lot anyway (parents like it when their child shows concern and courtesy). Don't forget to do a lot of chores. You know, like learning to wash your own clothes and stuff like that. Also ironing your own clothes and cleaning your room and you should take a bath every day (parents love it when you keep yourself clean). The best people to be extra nice to is your parents, grandparents, uncles and aunts, your mom and dad's friends, godfather, stepfather, cousins, brothers and sisters, great grandparents, and of course, close friends of the family. These most times will be some of your first customers.

Chapter Two

Offer Good deeds and Services to others

Most times you can find things around your neighborhood to earn money, such as shoveling snow, running errands for people in your neighborhoods, or just helping people with their groceries by carrying or delivering them to their homes.

You can even help the elderly by holding the door for them or helping them to cross the street safely. Sometimes people pay you, sometimes they'll just say "Thank you". But both are good because if you get paid, then you'll have money to spend or save, and if they say thank you, then you're storing up your blessings for good luck, which might transfer into money! People often remember when you do nice things for them and may decide to tip you the next time. I'm telling you, doing good deeds and getting the neighbors to know you, trust you, and to be able to depend on you can be very rewarding.

I remember the first time I offered to wash a neighbors' car. He saw how dirty his car was so he accepted my offer. When I was finished, he was so pleased with my work that he paid me $10 dollars for doing it. After that it was as if I had a job because he kept asking me to wash his car at least once a week. Then he told his friends and some of the neighbors on the block about my services and they all paid me to wash their cars. Now I was really getting paid! I also did other jobs like going to the store, running errands, shoveling snow in the winter and in the fall I would rake leaves, and boy was I raking in the bucks! I couldn't believe all the money I was making! I could have opened up my own "K.J.s' Odd Jobs & Services" Co.

So take from my experiences and apply them to your neighborhood and you'll see how quick you can earn money without even leaving the block. I guarantee it.

KJ'S Tip No. 1

Girls, if you know people on your block who have children, then you can offer to be their babysitter. They will pay you a certain amount of money to babysit their young children so that they won't have to be worried about the kids when they go out, and you won't have to worry anymore about money because now you have a job. But babysitting is a very responsible job;

First you have to be old enough to watch after someone else's children, needless to say your own brothers and sisters if you have any.

Second, you have to be a good babysitter which means you can't have parties or invite your friends over when the parents leave, or run up their phone bill (remember our discussion in chapter 1 about the bills), or do anything that they don't expect you to do unless you ask their permission.

You have to do your job well because they will tell other parents with children about you, which will mean more money!

Babysitting is a way to earn steady cash and also another way to get in closer with people from your area for other jobs. If you can't find anyone in your neighborhood that needs a babysitter, then ask your parents to help you place an ad in your local newspapers' 'Classified Section.' It's not expensive at all and it's also worth it.

It can be something short and simple like this:

NEED A BABYSITTER?
CALL 123-4567

That's all it takes! Just relax and prepare for your phone to start ringing off the hook with replies to your ad. Now all you have to do is choose the job that pays the best!

Sell your 'Unwanted Possessions' for profit

You can make money in several different ways. Do you remember when I talked about how you could sell your used toys, clothes and games? Well you can, easily, by setting up your very own mini flea market. Do you realize how many young children beg their parents daily to buy those action figures like G.I. Joe, Power Rangers and a dozen others that you may have piled up in a corner, collecting dust because you've outgrown them? But their parents often have to refuse them because number 1, they cost so much and number 2, their kids want all of them at one time!

Well, this is where you come in. If you have a bunch of old toys that you don't want anymore but are in good shape, you can sell them for less than half of the price that is in the store. You'd be surprised how quick a parent would come to you before they would go to Toys R Us or Kiddie City.

That's a sure way to get quick bucks. Also, if you have video games that you are no longer interested in, you could sell them too. I remember when I decided to sell my games. I sold them for less than half of what they originally cost. If it had cost $80 bucks, then I sold it for $25. I remember when I sold a game worth $60 dollars. I sold it for only $20. I'm telling you, these kids' parents jumped for joy when they saw low prices like that! Remember, they want to "<u>save</u>" money too, so when they see prices like yours, they rush to buy it. Everybody wants to save money, I mean **everybody**, so when you have something that people like, and you don't care for it anymore, sell it for cheap. I promise you they will come to you first before they ever see the shelves of the store.

***Note:** There are times when a parent won't be able to afford to pay and you may just have to give it to the child anyway because it's the right thing to do. It's called charity, and it's for people who are less fortunate and can't afford to pay, but that's a subject for another book.

KJ's Tips No. 2

If you want to make money while in school, buy a few packs of pens, pencils and paper and sell them to the students who need them. Put the change into your "special savings jar" as I'll talk about in the next chapter. Do not use this money. And remember to sell them for cheap so they will come back to buy from you. Just look at it this way, everyone in school has to write, right?"

Chapter Three

Money

How to Get and How to Save Money

Whenever I have any loose change, I make a habit of putting it in my jar where I save money. All my change gets put into it. Every day that I make change, every single cent, whenever. But you have to have the <u>discipline</u> not to touch it. Do not spend it on baseball cards or video games, gum, candy, just save it. You'll be surprised how much money you will have by the end of the year. So much that you won't even want to count it!

For instance, I remember when I first tried this method. I was totally shocked by how much money I saved! The jar filled up to the top! I knew I had to find someone in a hurry that I could trust, because I was not about to count that money alone. It would have taken hours on hours to get the job done; nevertheless, I eventually finished and came up with great results.

So you see, the method *does* work. Try it and I'll bet you can't count it all by yourself! Once you've reached a certain place where you have made quite a bit of money and you can spend some and still have a good amount leftover, then another way you can save money would be to open up a bank account. That way every time you get money you can spend half and save half and put it into the bank. If you get an allowance you can just hold onto it or tell your parents to put it in the bank for you.

The best way would be to have your parents hold your allowance for you because if they give it to you, you might begin to have second thoughts, because you might see something that you like, such as a video game, a toy, some new sneakers or you might want to spend it all on movies. After all of that you are going to have nothing left over, but if you save your money and put it in the bank, your money builds up, because the bank pays you something called "interest". This means if you leave your money in their bank, they will add to your money. And all the years add up. If you keep putting money into the bank and don't take any out you're going to have a lot of money. Try this method, it works.

*Note: Only take money out for emergencies.

Original drafts from 1995

Saving Method

Another way to save money is to cry broke. I'm only kidding, but I know of some people that use this method and it works for them. Even though they make a lot of money, they never seem to have any if you ask them for some. They say that they are "broke". But that's a quick way to be labelled "stingy" or a "cheapskate", which isn't always a good way to be. Sometimes it's good to share, but like I said before, that's for another book.

Anyway, when you get money, another method is to save half of it.

For example, if you have $5 dollars, then you put $2.50 of it away to the side. Then you will still have $2.50 to spend and do what you want to do with it. Even if you have $2.00 or $1.00, the same rule applies. Or, say if you have $2 dollars, you might spend $1.50 and save the remaining .50 cents. Just remember, if you have money and you break it down to half and you still have change leftover that you're not using, follow the beginning of this chapter and put it into your savings jar. I'm telling you it works.

Here are halves of money in case you don't know what half is .The first amount is what you have, the second amount is what you save:

$1.00= .50 $2.00=$1.00
$3.00=$1.50 $4.00=$2.00
$5.00=$2.50 $6.00=$3.00
$7.00=$3.50 $8.00=$4.00
$9.00=$4.50 $10.00=$5.00

and so on. Just save half of whatever you have. If you still don't know what half is, "You'd better ask somebody!" But you should know if you can read this book.

Don't forget to save that change!

Chapter Four

How to Spend and Save your Money

"DON'T WASTE YOUR MONEY ON JUNK. SAVE IT FOR WHEN YOU REALLY NEED IT."

I know that everyone would like to save money, especially children because they hardly get any; but when they do, they spend it all up foolishly on things like toys and junk food. If you want to keep (save) money you can't go to the store and spend it all on junk food, because first of all, too much junk food is no good for you, in fact *no* junk food is good for you, but if you *must* have it, cut down on it. The reason I say cut down is because I know it is impossible for a child to stop eating all junk foods, so I say cut down; then you'll have money in your pockets for something that you really want, or you can just save the money.

You can also save money by not buying up a whole lot of toys. Of course some toys, but not so many. I know every child out there loves to play with toys, but if you've reached the age where you want to have money, you'll quit buying so many of them.

My grandmother always says "everything in moderation" which means don't overdo anything, because "too much of anything is no good". She'd also say "If you can't eat it, then don't spend money on junk like that", and she meant real food, not junk food.

Since we're on the subject of spending and saving money, I thought I might suggest to you the right way to buy your clothes. *Catch sales!!* 'Sale' is the key word. If you like something and it's on sale, I say get it. *You're saving* money, *and you're getting what you want.* Remember when I talked about selling something for a cheaper price then

what your originally bought if for? Well if
you see something in the store that's less
than the original price, *go for it!*

Chapter Five

How to Use, Save and be Smart with your Money

How to Keep Money

Just because you're making money now doesn't mean you go spend it all at once; you save it. If you have food and drinks in your home, then you don't need to buy anything like that from the store with your money. You're not supposed to spend money just because you have it. Another way to keep money is to be a little frugal. What I mean is, buy some $20 dollar or $25 dollar pants and some $5 dollar shirts. You can still buy name brand sneakers, but you don't have to buy the newest sneakers on the market. For example, I went to Newark, New Jersey and bought a pair of *K-Swiss* sneakers. They're not even a major name brand and everyone was walking up to me and saying "Oh wow KJ! Those sneakers are phat!"

Now I'm saying to myself all along that they're not even name brand, but people like them! And the good thing about it is that I'm not paying $50, $60, or $70 dollars for them either!

Another thing is that you don't buy your clothes; most time your parents' do, so remember, the best way to get the clothes you want is to do well in school and get a good report card. Also, behave at home and treat everyone extra nice by being courteous, so that when you go school shopping for clothes, you can get the clothes that you pick out because you've been good, and your parents will see that you've earned and deserve it. That's how you get good things. Make a good habit of remembering to ask before you leave the house if anyone needs anything from the store as I mentioned before. And don't forget to complete all your chores around the house. This combined with good grades in school will make it a cinch for you to get what you want when the time comes.

But remember what to do with your money. Put it away. Save it even for later years if you can. If you save for 5 years straight you'll have well over a few thousand dollars for something that you really need. Spend money when you need something. Remember there is a difference between need and want. And if you need something, before using your money, ask your parents to buy it for you. If you need it they shouldn't say no. But its things that you may want such as games and lot of other material things that you might have trouble convincing your parents to buy. Remember be smart with your money. Use it wisely. Save it and don't spend it all up

Holding onto Your Savings

Crying broke is one of the best ways to keep your savings. I know I said earlier that I was kidding, and this may sound funny and you may even laugh, but if anyone ask you if you have any money, just learn to say "No", unless it is an emergency or you just have extra money in your pocket to spare, otherwise do not dig into your savings. My dad advises me to keep a little money set aside for the needy, in case someone just needs a little help. He says we all need help from time to time, so I make it a habit to keep just a little extra money, so in case someone asks, I won't feel like I'm digging into my savings. Also, never bring any of your savings out with you all at once, anything can happen. Keep it in a safe place like a hiding spot or in the best place for it, a bank.

How to Use your Savings

Do you know how to use your savings? If you do, then you don't. Don't use them, that is. You only use your savings for emergencies or when you want to maybe open a business of your own to make more money or to make an investment. That is if you're like me and want to become wealthy some day.

Chapter Six

Keeping track of your Money

"MONEY GOES SO FAST, IT'S HARD TO KEEP UP WITH IT!"

Throughout this book I've talked about how to earn, save and keep money, but I never discussed how to keep track of your money. Keeping track of your money means knowing how much you have and how much you've spent. A good way to keep track of your money is to have a money calendar on which you would mark down everyday how much you've spent. Whatever you have left over of course goes into your savings. At the end of the month, you would add up all the money you've spent and what you've saved. That way you'll know how much you have.

This brings me to a story:

"Not long ago there were two young boys who lived in the city. One was wealthy and had every and anything he wanted. The other boy was from a below average income family that was not as fortunate and had to struggle for everything he got. The boy that was wealthy thought that since he had a lot of money that he could spend it all up without having to keep conscious of his spending, while on the other hand the boy that didn't really have much saved and kept track of his money." "Months and months went by.

One day the wealthy boy went into the bank to take out money so that he and a couple of friends could go to the mall. But what he didn't know was that all the money that he kept taking out of the bank decreased what he had in his savings and left him bankrupt!! On the other hand, the other boy continuously put money in his savings account and "kept track" of his money and found out that he had enough money to take care of him and his family for many years to come."

"In conclusion, the two boys actually switched places from the beginning of the story til the end of the story. The reason for this is because the wealthy boy was not focused, and didn't have the discipline and most of all he didn't keep track of his money."

So follow the steps of the boy who is now wealthy from applying the principles of saving. You'll find great satisfaction.

FIGURE 1: A chart on "How to keep track of money"

	HOW MUCH I HAVE	HOW MUCH I SPENT	HOW MUCH I SAVED	TOTAL SAVED
MON	$20	$5	$15	$15
TUES	10	4	6	6
WED	12	6	6	6
THURS	9	7	2	2
FRI	25	14	11	11
SAT	15	5	10	10
SUN	8	3	5	5

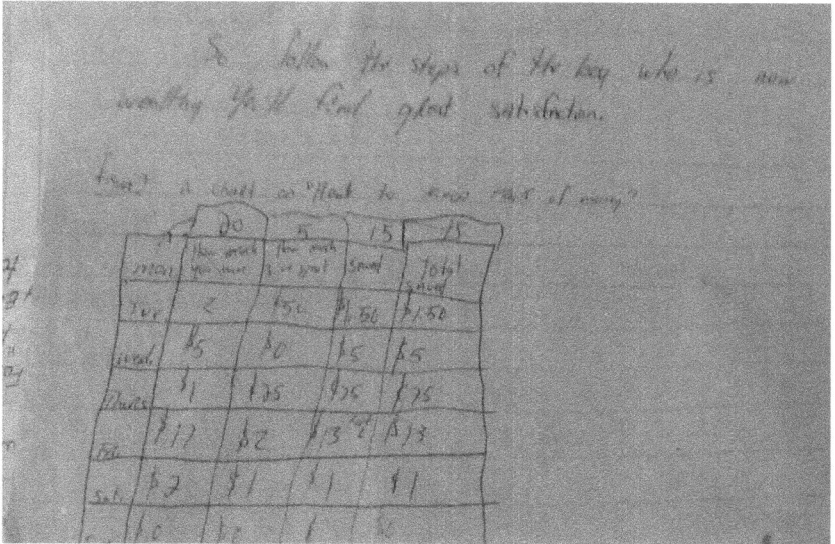

Chapter Seven

Keeping Organized

Don't let money get in the way of your priorities. If you have homework, then do it first before you think about making money. That's what I do. Be organized. Go according to a schedule from when you wake up until you go to bed. When you're organized, then nothing can fall out of place. You know that when you come home from school, the first thing you should do is your homework. Since you're mind is still in school mode, why not do your homework? I'm talking about right away, not 30 minutes later, but as soon as you come in, because if you wait too long you might want to do something else.

After you finish you homework, then look around the house to see if anything needs to be straightened up. Do your chores.

If you need to clean your room, then do it! It shouldn't take long because since you're organized, then you would know just where everything belongs. When you're done, then you can now follow your plans to make some cash. When I go according to a schedule it usually takes no longer than an hour and a half. Most of that time is spent doing homework, but once I have that out of the way, then I have time for my friends or anything else that I may want to do. You just keep repeating the same thing over and over everyday, because now you're organized and going according to a schedule. A <u>schedule</u> helps you to stay on track, and helps you to complete things that need to be done, which is the main purpose of keeping organized.

Try going according to a schedule for a few weeks and you will see just how much your life will change for the better. I guarantee it.

Chapter Eight

Planning and Setting Goals

Planning is very important when you're trying to save money. If you don't have the training, then you can't save because you won't have the discipline, and would keep going into your savings to take out money, not for important things, but just because you have some. A good way to plan is to focus on goals. You have to say to yourself something like, "How much money do I want to earn in 4 years?" If you set the goal, then you have to work towards that goal and make sure that you reach the exact amount or more than what you planned. This not only applies to saving money, this can apply to almost anything you do.

For example; in school, if you set a goal and say that in 2 years you're going to make straight A's on your report card, then that means that everyday in school you must work up to your fullest potential to make sure that you get those A's, right? Well it's the same with money. If you set a goal saying that in 3 years you are going to save up to $3000 dollars, then you're going to have to work hard in order to make sure you have at least that amount or more by that set time. Get the picture? But you must have a plan in order to get there. Set long term goals and set out to accomplish them. When you finally do, you'll feel great about yourself and what you've accomplished.

But try to set goals that you will complete. Be realistic about your goals and don't forget to write them down. Don't try keeping all the information in your head because you will forget. Keep a well written plan out where you can see it. It's like my dad always tells me, "*He who fails to plan, plans to fail.*

Chapter Nine

Proper Attitude

"WHAT'S THE BIG IDEA? THAT'S THE SAME TOY *I* TRIED TO SELL YOU!"

Having a proper attitude about selling is important. The way a person acts can have an affect on how they attract money. The one who has a positive attitude towards working hard to earn money will usually become successful because first of all, they enjoy the idea of making money. It doesn't feel like work at all because they're having fun while they're doing it, such as selling, saving, keeping focused and practicing sticking to their schedules at school and at home. They enjoy kicking their old habits for their new better ones because now from experience they know they'll get rewarded in the end.

On the other hand, the person with a negative attitude hardly ever has success because they may not enjoy the work. They may be lazy and may not believe in themselves due to low self esteem and low confidence, which makes them believe that they won't be any good at selling or making money even before they start. Therefore, the person with the positive attitude usually winds up making all the bucks.

If you want to be successful in making money, you can't have a quitter's attitude because that's just what happens, you already believe that you won't make money, and quit before you even try.

I used to have that attitude. I remember when I first started selling goods to make money, things weren't going my way. It was 8:00 in the evening and I didn't make a single cent all day. The worst thing about it was that I started out at 9:00 in the morning (it was a Saturday). I would go to customers and try to sell them something, but they would tell me "No thanks" or "try back later." After a while I got discouraged and didn't want to sell anymore. I wanted to quit and find something else to do with my time, but something inside me told me to keep on going and not to give up.

I convinced myself that I could do it, to just keep on trying. Then all of a sudden something happened. I made a sale! After that my attitude started to change, and I started smiling more and I noticed that people started to buy again and again. That night I actually wound up selling 12 items!

So as you can see, you have to have faith and the proper attitude about selling because it can help you when you feel like the world is over and it's time to give up. You must always remember, *"A quitter never wins and a winner never quits."* I know I will.

Paper Attitude

The way a person Acts also can have an effect on how they attract money. A person with a positive Attitude towards working hard to get money could become successful in doing so because they Enjoy the idea of making money. It doesn't feel like hard work to them because they'll having fun while their doing it (selling, saving, keeping focus, sticking to their schedule for in school and at home etc.) They enjoy kicking their old (bad) habits for their new (better) ones because they know that

Original drafts from 1995

Building Confidence

A way a person Acts Alke can have an effect on how they Attrack money. A Person with A Positive Attitude About working hard to get money could become successful in doing so. While A person with a bad attitude

Chapter Ten

Building Confidence

As I mentioned in the last chapter, a proper and positive attitude is important in selling if you want to be successful. When I said that a person with a negative attitude may be lazy and lack confidence, on the other hand, a person with a positive one usually works twice as hard and gets the positive results because of his high self esteem and high level of confidence. It makes him feel like he can accomplish anything he puts his mind to, so he just does it with pleasure. His attitude shows in his actions.

For example, Option_*1*: say that a person approaches you with a bright attitude and is neatly dressed and asks if you would like to purchase a product from them, would you most likely buy it? Or, Option_*2*: would you buy something from someone less pleasant? Who is dressed poorly with their clothes hanging off of them, smells bad and doesn't speak properly and looks like they might've stolen what they're selling to you?

I know you are smart so you probably chose *Option 1*. As quick as you just answered that question is how quick a person would rather buy from you if you were like *Option 1* too.

Now some people just may not have an aggressive kind of personality, so if you find that you're one of those people who just lack confidence, then do what I did. Ask your parents to enroll you into a martial arts class. You might be thinking; "Yeah, right. Now all that kicking and acting crazy like

Bruce lee is not going to help my confidence or anything else", right? Wrong!! It will! Martial Arts is not just for self-defense, it is a part of life, which means it helps to build your confidence, character, and discipline while also learning how to defend yourself against attackers.

If you want to build up your confidence and do it quickly, just train hard in class so when tournaments come up, maybe your teacher may decide to enter you. Now in case you're wondering "What's a tournament?" Well, it's an event where students from schools all over come to display their skills, and to perform various tasks in the arts such as fighting, which is also referred to as sparring or *Kumite* (which *really* helps to build your confidence and character), weapons, forms better known as *Kata*, and self-defense techniques.

I remember my first tournament. I had to fight 5 times just to win a trophy. Having to fight that many times didn't only give me the victory, but it built up confidence in me, which made me want to keep on going. Winning feels great, and that's what Karate does. It gives you the confidence not to quit and to keep on trying.

So even if I'm trying to make sales and I'm having a bad or slow day, a day where I haven't made a dime and the day is almost gone, what I've learned in the martial arts gives me the confidence and discipline to finish the whole day out without quitting. Sometimes I make money and sometimes I don't, but I never give up until I finish the day. That is the main thing because if you give up, then you'll never know what you could have accomplished.

I know a lot of parents are afraid of sending their children to karate school for two reasons: Either they are afraid that their child might get hurt, or they think that once their child knows karate they might become bullies and pick fights. Well, as long as you're trained by a qualified teacher, then he will teach the right way so that you won't get hurt. He will also instill the discipline in you that makes you not to go out and pick fights with other people just because you can now defend yourself. That takes a lot of discipline and like I was saying before, you need to have a lot of discipline to save money too. So if karate teaches you discipline, then there's your proof that it is not only for self-defense, but a way of life.

So you see how important your behavior is to the things you do in life. It can help you to become successful.

Chapter Eleven

Moral Behavior

If you want to become more successful in earning money, good moral behavior is a must. Do you know what moral behavior is? Well instead of looking at the glossary in the back of a book, I'll tell you. Moral Behavior is like manners. It's your ability to distinguish between right and wrong. For example, if you know that you have the opportunity to steal from or take advantage of someone without being caught, but you don't, then that's an example of a person who's honest and has good morals. Another example would be if you know that your friends are up to no good and your conscious tells you not to be influenced by the crowd and you walk away, then that also shows good judgment and good conduct. That is good moral behavior.

Ways to develop Good Moral Behavior

One way you can develop good morals is to believe and put God first in your life, because without him, there would be no you, or such a thing as money to be able to earn. Going to church, the temple, or however you worship God, is a good way to be reminded of how he wants us to be and act towards one another. We have to put into practice what we're taught about good. You could participate in community activities, and get in the habit of doing good deeds for others. By listening to our parents and doing well in school as well as at home, are good ways to stay on a good track. Try hard to get A's at home as well as in school. Don't get all A's in school and F's at home. Be mindful of doing your chores, and taking care of responsibilities around the house as well. I always listen to my father when he tells me to do something, but like every child, I sometimes make mistakes too. It's normal for a person to make errors, so don't be afraid if you make a mistake; it's a part of growing up.

I remember when I was ten years old. My father always gave me books to read and he would tell me to summarize each chapter that I read. For some strange reason he always wanted me to write. He would tell me at times that one day *"it"* would all *"click"*. Now you're probably saying what I said three years ago, "What does he mean by *"click"*?" Don't feel bad. I didn't know what he meant by it either; However I do remember when he would say if you do something over and over, that it will eventually become natural to you. So as time went by, I continued to write and write. When I reached the age of thirteen I finally figured out what "click" meant. My father was right, because here I am today writing a book. "Oh yeah!" It must have "clicked"!" What my dad meant by click

Original drafts from 1995

was that if I kept on writing, one day it would become easy and natural to me.

The lesson in this is to show how important it is to listen to your parents or anyone who's in authority over you that means you well, for example, your teachers.

If I hadn't listened, I would not have known that I had writing skills. Remember, listening to your parents and those who love and care for you help you to develop good morals, and helps you to become a noble person which are important characteristics you need to earn money.

I am taught to give all praise and credit to God and I am thankful for my father for making it interesting for me to listen and to be obedient, and for making me happy and satisfied with what I do. You can do something great too and make your parents proud of you.

K.J.'s tips # 3

Whenever something good happens to you in life, give thanks to God to show your appreciation, and to show that you're thankful for what *he* has done for you.

Chapter Twelve

Beware of Greed

I know that I talk a lot about making money in this book, but that's because it's just what this book is about, however, beware not to get caught up into making money so much that you forget about people and begin to get so excited with your progress that you start to mistreat people, especially those close to you. Don't get big headed, that's a quick way to lose friends and respect. Make sure you remember to keep a leveled head and don't neglect the important things you have to do.

So read this book, take your time and follow my advice, and step by step, slowly but surely you will be rewarded, God willing.

Good luck!

Khalis J. Harris- Age 32, 2014

Dad & Khalis J. Harris, age 13, Graduation pic 1995

Check out More Titles from our

W.O.M.B. PUBLICATIONS' Authors!

What We do in Preschool

Zakiyah's "My Big Happy Family"

Life after Death: Remembering Shamuda

by Desiree' Monique

- also-

We Have a Problem: Let's Solve it!
by Rimma Mello

The Takeoff Show Comic Book
by Mikal Harris

For Orders visit our website at:

www.wombpublications.com

For info contact:

Raymond Harris- Editor in Chief

W.O.M.B. Publications

Giving Birth to the Best Books on Earth!

www.ingramcontent.com/pod-product-compliance
Lightning Source LLC
Chambersburg PA
CBHW070109070426
42448CB00038B/2388